Divorc

Remarriage

*Policy Options and Pastoral Guidelines
for Church Leaders*

Robert Warren

National Officer for Evangelism

Formerly Team Rector, St Thomas' Church,
Crookes, Sheffield

GROVE BOOKS LIMITED
BRAMCOTE NOTTINGHAM NG9 3DS

Contents

Acknowledgements

I want to acknowledge the patience, understanding and teamwork behind this booklet. It could not have been done without the hard thinking and praying of Paddy Mallon (Baptist Minister), Derek Frank, John Davies and Mark Stibbe (Anglican clergy), and the stimulating contribution of Steve Williams, one of the leaders of the Nine O'Clock Service, who also helped in the writing of the early drafts of part of this material.

I also want to record my thanks to Bishop Kenneth Skelton (chairman of the General Synod's *Marriage and the Church's Task* report) for his helpful comments that have protected the manuscript from some of its worst errors. His insight and knowledge were freely given, though he would not want to endorse all of the arguments put forward in this booklet.

The work behind this booklet could not have been done without the willingness of a loving and thoughtful Church Council to wrestle with their own consciences, the teaching of Scripture, and the human stories that refused to fit into neat categories. It would have been much the poorer without the willingness of church members who had been divorced to face again the pain of the past in working alongside us in this matter. Even our final decision was a pain to some. I honour them for keeping journeying with us.

This booklet is offered as a contribution to the whole church, to stimulate its thinking and action in these matters.

The Cover Illustration is by Roger Gibson

First Impression September 1992
Reprinted April 1995
ISSN 0144-171X
ISBN 1 85174 219 0

1
Context Issues

Introduction

A knock on the vicarage door, or a telephone call, produces the straightforward statement 'We would like to get married at your church.'

Clergy have learned to develop a simple procedure which gets the various forms filled up, ensures that the banns are read, that preparation is done as effectively as possible within the time constraints of a thousand other pastoral priorities and that the marriage service is a 'day to remember'—for the right reasons!

However, increasingly these days, if clergy have not learned to forestall the issues, a further piece of information is slipped in innocently: 'One of us is divorced; does that make any difference?'

What was a routine enquiry immediately becomes a complex pastoral problem. Behind that question so many issues and people and problems, and so much pain, are usually to be found. This booklet seeks to supply answers at two levels. First, it sets out a framework within which clergy, Church Council and other lay leaders involved, can make decisions about what form of service to offer. Second, it gives practical pastoral guidelines about how to help those recovering from the trauma of divorce. Arguably it is the second that matters most, yet it is the former ('Can we get married in church?') which is usually top of the agenda for the couple concerned.

It needs to be stated what this booklet is not about. It is not an attempt to explore, in depth, the theoretical backgrounds to such decisions and practices. Others have done that. Rather, this booklet is produced for clergy and leaders at the 'sharp end' of the problem, that is, those who have to make pastoral decisions, even when the scholars are not agreed about the Matthaean exception!

Nor is the booklet designed primarily for those who have experienced divorce. Again, others have written helpfully on this subject. Rather, this booklet is designed to help those who have to make decisions about, and give pastoral help to, those who have been divorced.

Such a booklet, seeking to address questions of 'what should we do about...?' is needed since the many issues associated with the remarriage of people who have been divorced are increasingly before the church today. Moreover, divorce is often a catalyst to faith as the shock waves of the experience shake the foundations of a person's life and call into question the values and priorities by which they have been living. The church, not least in a decade of evangelism, can expect to find a considerable number of divorced people seeking to enter its membership. Their continuing presence will undoubtedly put this matter on the agenda of most churches.

St Thomas's Church, Crookes, in Sheffield is one such church that has had to address the issue. What follows is the material which formed the basis of discussion in the staff team and at the level of Church Council. It is shared with the wider church in the hope that the work we did may help others.

Although the particular policy that we have adopted, and the reasons for doing so, are given, the aim of this small contribution is to spell out a number of different options. It is quite possible that some will find this document helpful in enabling them to develop a different solution to the one we arrived at. Certainly much of the material about counselling is relevant whatever policy option is adopted.

A word needs to be addressed at this point about the particular situation out of which this material arose, which illustrates why it may speak to a wide cross-section of churches.

St Thomas's Church is a parish church dealing, like most, with the routine requests for marriage both from its own members and from the local community. It is also a Local Ecumenical Project comprising Anglicans and Baptists. This has meant finding a policy that can encompass both the 'gathered church' approach of Baptists as well as the parochial responsibility of Anglicans. As a large church (with over one thousand worshippers) the issues about the remarriage of divorced people come up regularly. Each one is unique, but after dealing with the twentieth or thirtieth one you do begin to see significant patterns emerging. The church is also a team ministry (with five clergy) which adds another complicating factor in handling this issue.

St Thomas's Church covers a wide cultural spectrum. The parish is the meeting point of three parliamentary constituencies. It is an area in the process of change reflected in the make-up of the congregation which, although predominantly middle-class, also includes people from a working-class background. Moreover, as a result of the development of a radical young urban adult congregation (The Nine O'Clock Service) the church also includes people from the so-called 'underclass.' It has challenged us to think again about what is 'gospel' and what is 'culture.' We have had to face the quite different dynamics involved in the break-up of marriage in 'underclass,' 'working-class' and 'middle-class' situations.

These problems can be described in the following way. Stress on marriages in the 'underclass culture' arise in the very earliest years (indeed months), as a result of childhood experiences of abuse, abandonment and insecurity. The problems arise at the point of 'knowing who I am,' and the basics of how to make a relationship. Sadly some such marriages never seem to start. The problem lies in making a relationship. In the working-class culture there is a higher degree of stability, but problems emerge in the free, and sometimes over-free (extravagant and blaming), expression of emotions. Such 'freedom' can sometimes end in the need and desire to destroy, or to control, the partner.

Marriage looks calmer in the middle-class culture but often only on the surface. Here the problems are typically related to an inability to get in touch with real feelings and a sense of shame associated with asking for help. When desperation overcomes a hiding of the problems it is often too late to be able to help.

For all these reasons it is likely that what we have wrestled with may well connect with a wide audience. This booklet is offered in the hope that it may help those currently addressing the issue to find their way through to a consistent, workable, holy and loving policy in handling the trauma of divorce.

It needs to be stated that the problem we faced was primarily that of remarriage for the divorced *within the church*. We then sought to work out how to bring our 'parish policy' into line with that within the limits of our Anglican legal requirements. The central question we addressed was 'what should the church's response be to the presence of divorced members seeking the church's blessing on the contracting of a second marriage?' If our situation had been such that most requests for remarriage after divorce had come from the local community we should no doubt have started from a different perspective. Whether the end conclusion of such wrestling would have been different it is impossible to say.

The Social Context

One of the greatest social changes in this country this century has been the greatly increased option of divorce. Economically it is now possible for a woman to be divorced. Legally divorce has become much easier to obtain. Socially, much of the stigma of divorce has disappeared. Other factors have contributed to the increase of divorce. Greater life expectancy leads to greater life expectancy for marriage. When many marriages did not survive fifteen years (because of the death of one of the partners) a number of the long-term strains did not appear. Furthermore, the change from 'procreation' to 'companionship' as the primary goal of marriage has raised expectations about the quality of the relationship (see *Marriage, Faith and Love* by Jack Dominian for a helpful introduction to the implications of 'companionship marriage'). With that has come an increase in failed expectations leading to abandonment of the marriage.

However, divorce is not a new issue for the church. It has been debated throughout the Christian era. The Early Fathers considered it in some detail, as did the Reformers. The Church of England, after all, was formed to a considerable extent out of the issue of divorce (that of Henry VIII). Divorce has been written about extensively in the Orthodox tradition as well. This debate over the centuries would not have taken place if the issue was purely theoretical. It is important to note that the wide range of understandings about how the church should respond which is around today have their roots in the tradition of the Christian church going back to earliest times. A brief history of this debate within the whole spectrum of the Christian era is helpfully set out in sections 141-159 in *Marriage and the Church's Task*.

Divorce is always a painful experience, and the church's first task is to speak (by word and action) of God's attitude of grace and mercy for those who go through this trauma. Discipline is appropriate where believers act contrary to Scripture but, even when true guilt is involved, the church needs also to minister to the self-doubt, sense of rejection, shame and complete disorientation that is usually involved in divorce. In particular, it is important to avoid the use of the label 'divorced' as a means of giving identity to a person. It describes what has happened to a person; it should never be used to define who they are.

It is important to bear in mind that handling the consequences of the breakdown of a marriage is only one part of the church's care of the institution of marriage. Moreover, marriage support is only one aspect of the church's overall pastoral care. This booklet seeks to bear in mind the time constraints on the normal clergyman and local church, and attempts to suggest options that are workable without dropping everything else, in the total mission of the church, to deal with this one issue.

The Church Context

There is considerable variation in the way that different denominations deal with the issue of divorce and remarriage.

The *Anglican* church has had several major debates since 1945. In the course of its debate of the report *Marriage and the Church's Task* (published in 1978, and debated in the following four years) General Synod came to the conclusion that there were certain circumstances in which the remarriage of divorced people could take place in church. However, it subsequently failed to reach any agreement about what those circumstances were, who should decide, on what grounds, and whether any particular couple fitted this principle.

The whole situation became somewhat confused. The earlier Convocation regulations (from the 1930s) had said that remarriage after divorce was not right within the church. However, the church had not sought to change the law of the land. Clergy of the Church of England are legally registrars and therefore have the authority to conduct the marriage of anyone whose marriage is acceptable in the law. To this unclear situation the church has now added the decision in principle to agree to remarriage—together with the failure in practice to find a workable way of achieving this.

This situation gives freedom to adopt any policy, from the 'highly rigorist' to the 'very open' position. Anecdotal evidence suggests a fairly widespread reluctance to practise any easy access to marriage after divorce. However, I have no firm statistics to support this assertion.

In *Non-conformist* churches there is at least as wide a range of policies as is found within the established church. Although largely congregational in the form of church government, there are national policies and patterns. The range of practices can be expressed by stating that whilst Baptist ministers are least likely to conduct marriage services for those who have been divorced, Methodist ministers are most likely to.

The *Catholic* and *Orthodox* churches have also wrestled with this subject over many centuries, and have developed their own distinctive ways of dealing with the problem.

The sobering fact is that although churches have adopted a variety of approaches to this issue, no church has come up with a policy that is so self-evidently right that any other church has been sufficiently convinced to change its policy in line with that 'one right way.' This booklet is not attempting to provide such a way. Rather, the more limited goal is to find a 'least bad' solution that has some good chance of being workable.

Before engaging with specific policy options, our starting point must be consideration of the biblical material which needs to inform and shape all our thinking. To that we turn next. I do so well aware that all the crucial texts have been hotly debated over most of the two millennia of the church's history. It is a dangerous minefield to enter, yet some summary and conclusions must be drawn if any attempt is to be made to establish a theological basis.

The Biblical Context

The *Old Testament* presents a remarkably complex and fluid picture. Although, from a Western perspective, polygamy seems to be at odds with the picture of marriage as a permanent, intimate union between a man and a woman, there is no censure of those who did practise it. What is clear is that marriage was seen as a 'creation ordinance' (Genesis 2.18-25) for all people. The emphasis in Genesis (underlined in negative form by the seventh commandment) is on the total social process of leaving home and establishing a new marriage community ('leaving and cleaving').

That monogamy emerges as the norm may have been due to the impact of such prophets as Hosea who saw the parallels between God's covenant with Israel and the marriage covenant. Certainly monogamy seems a more appropriate form of marriage to arise out of a monotheistic theology.

However, the Old Testament presents a complex marriage picture in which the isolation of a man and woman, plus their children, into the modern nuclear family is far from the norm. The extended household and tribe no doubt resulted in a significantly different experience of what marriage means from today's world. The economic and social constraints on women largely ruled out any functioning as a one-parent family. The book of Ruth provides a fascinating commentary on both the isolation, and yet community support, of such a family.

Although the lifelong monogamous ideal seems to emerge, it is also made clear that, since the fall, human beings have lived on a less than ideal level. The Bible recognizes this, and so, in Deuteronomy 24, there are brief guidelines that govern the practice of divorce, a practice that is tolerated, but never commanded or divinely encouraged.

According to the Old Testament, divorce was legal, permanent and permissible only when 'uncleanness' was involved. This led to a debate among Jewish scholars as to whether this included any inappropriate behaviour, or just sexual infidelity. Jesus clearly sided with those who held a high view of marriage.

The *teaching of Jesus* upheld the permanent nature of marriage, pointed out that divine permission for divorce had only been given because of human sinfulness, stated that sexual immorality was a legitimate cause for divorce, and clearly taught that the one who divorces a sexually faithful partner and marries another commits adultery.

Jesus was particularly addressing the injustice to women in that culture. They could be divorced without any rights, often for trivial reasons, but were not able themselves to divorce their husband. He said that divorce was not God's original or best will, but that it was nevertheless given by God because 'your hearts were hard' (Matthew 19.8). Sadly, our hearts are still hard today, and divorce is sometimes the consequence.

We need to acknowledge the impact of modern scholarship on our understanding of the biblical material. The majority of scholars would question whether the Matthaean exception clause ('except for the case of adultery') is original to Jesus. They point to the Gospel of Mark as the earlier gospel and see Matthew's addition as just that—Matthew's addition. Others have argued that the mention of adultery was to give an example of the sort of seriousness of sin that merits a permissible divorce, rather than to make one unique exception.

Finally, it is necessary to comment on the question of whether, as far as the teaching of Jesus is concerned, remarriage (as distinct from divorce) is permissible. Jesus's teaching about divorce speaks specifically about one who 'marries another,' and its natural interpretation is that that is a possibility opened up by divorce (Mt 19.9). In the same passage (Mt 19.1-12) Jesus speaks about the call to single life as a Kingdom life-style. We need to point people to that and help them to recognize the possibility of God's call to that, and to give them support in it. But to require it as law is to change the whole biblical dynamic of the Kingdom from calling and grace to law and regulation. Jesus warned that that could not be done: 'not everyone can accept this word, but only those to whom it has been given' (Mt 19.11). In my judgment this represents a further implicit recognition of the possibility of remarriage.

The *teaching of Paul* adds a second permissible cause for divorce, namely desertion by the unbelieving partner. He instructs Christians to let their unbelieving partner go, if that partner wishes to divorce them because they have become believers. Paul is not encouraging the believer to take the initiative in divorcing their partner. Rather he is advising the believer not to fight divorce in these circumstances. The implication is that a person taking this advice would remain in good standing with the church. Paul also urged the unmarried to stay single. However, the specific context of this teaching suggests that this advice may well have been related to the harsh persecution the church was facing as Paul wrote.

As far as the possibility of remarriage after divorce is concerned, Paul's teaching about Christians being divorced for their faith specifically includes the possibility of remarriage: 'a believing man or woman is not bound in such circumstances' (1 Cor 7.15).

In the *contemporary church*, a further ground for divorce has gained ground, particularly within the pentecostal/charismatic tradition. This has been called the 'new creation' view. This teaches that when a person comes to faith they are released from the past in such a full sense that the slate is wiped clean and marriages contracted, and broken, before faith are part of the past which God forgives. In such a situation, where divorce took place before a person came to faith then remarriage would be permissible.

It seems an attractive expression of the power of the gospel to 'make all things new.' However, it needs to be treated with some caution since it is such a novelty in terms of the church's approach to divorce. It remains a way of seeing remarriage that has little precedent in the tradition of the church outside the twentieth century, or the pentecostal/charismatic tradition (unless the Catholic practice, in Africa for example, of considering marriage prior to baptism as not a true marriage, forms some sort of historical precedent). At best, this view is a derived or secondary argument that is of a different order from the clearly defined principles spelt out in the teaching of Jesus and Paul.

Beyond the immediate texts about marriage and divorce, the Scriptures introduce great themes such as holiness, grace, covenant, forgiveness and justice which all have a profound bearing on decisions that have to be made about how to handle those who have been divorced. All too easily, when a clergyman is dealing with an actual situation it seems that justice and mercy fight each other. Seeing how they might kiss each other is indeed a difficult task.

Conclusions

The following *conclusions* can be drawn from the above material:
(a) God intended marriage to be a permanent and exclusive union between a man and a woman, who find their sexual fulfilment within marriage.
(b) Divorce is nowhere commanded in Scripture and neither is it encouraged.
(c) No Christian should aggressively seek the dissolution of their marriage.
(d) In extreme cases, against the wishes and efforts of the committed partner, if the marriage bond is destroyed beyond human ability to restore it, God, in his grace and as a concession to human weakness, allows divorce.

   I used to think that no Christian should ever initiate a divorce. However, I have now seen from the experience of church members that there are circumstances where it has seemed right to advise a Christian to initiate divorce proceedings.
(e) Both Jesus and Paul speak of a positive vision for the single life see Matthew 19 and 1 Corinthians 7. Such a life, dedicated to the Lord, is not a second best to marriage but is as high a calling. It is good to communicate this both by the way we affirm and give responsibility to those called to such a life, and also as part of the church's presenting the options to those facing life after marriage. It is important to remember that the only truly whole person who ever

lived experienced that wholeness as a single person.

However, there are problems with the biblical evidence:

(a) It says nothing about how to treat or discipline those who are divorced.

(b) It says nothing about homes filled with violence, physical and mental abuse, deviant forms of behaviour, failure to provide for a family's physical well-being, alcoholism, a refusal to let other members of the family worship, or a variety of other destructive influences.

(c) It says nothing about marriage services, let alone services of remarriage.

Divorce is expressly permitted in cases of adultery, and if the unbelieving partner wishes to be divorced. In these cases remarriage is permitted either indirectly, or directly (Mt 19.9 and 1 Cor 7.15).

Finally, in considering the biblical material, it is important to recognize the danger of handling the Scriptures in a legalistic way. The heart of the argument which Jesus had with the Scribes and Pharisees was that they wanted everything to be expressed in terms of law so that they could control their relationship to God and the behaviour of others. Jesus, in proclaiming the kingdom, pointed to another way of seeing reality—the way of grace rather than law.

With the best will in the world, and with the best intentions, the moment we look at the teaching of Jesus in order to establish rules for marriage after divorce we are confining the Kingdom within a legal perspective. The task of making decisions about how to deal with people who are seeking to be married after they have been divorced must be tackled. However, the more we can do so aware of the dangers of legalism, the better we are likely to do the job.

In the light of all the above, we identified three biblical grounds for divorce, with the possibility of remarriage.

a) *Adultery* The 'exception clause' in Matthew 19 ('except for the cause of unfaithfulness') is a basis within the teaching of Jesus for divorce. Notwithstanding the questions raised by scholars about the authenticity of the Matthaean exception, I conclude that Scripture, as we have received it, is to be taken as authoritative in the life of the church.

b) *Desertion* Paul's teaching in 1 Cor 7 is the basis of this principle.

c) *'New creation'* Though not of the same biblical foundation as the above two arguments, the 'new creation' argument points to the possibility of marriage when the previous marriage, and subsequent divorce, took place before the person came to faith.

2

Policy Options

Framework for a policy

In considering the options for handling the marriage of those who have been divorced we found it helpful to set them out in a tabulated form (see figure 1). This gave us a framework within which we could not only choose what seemed the best way, but also do so aware of the options which we were thereby setting aside.

The top line identifies three broad categories of divorce. These are as follows. First, the *biblical* category. This covers the three grounds of divorce identified at the end of chapter 1 above.

Next comes the *extra-biblical* category. This covers those circumstances where remarriage, though it cannot be argued directly from Scripture, yet seems to require sympathetic treatment—for example, physical abuse of spouse or children. Although Scripture does not explicitly allow divorce in such situations, it does seem in harmony with the Bible's teaching about defence of the weak and powerless. Seeking to help and protect those who are victims of hostile behaviour by others may—in some circumstances—necessitate divorce. It also includes the situation of those divorced against their will.

The third category, *contra-biblical*, is intended to cover situations where Scripture seems to support a judgment against divorce. This includes situations where someone has committed adultery or deserted their partner simply because 'I no longer love him/her,' or because 'I want a change' and so on.

Down the left side of the table are listed five possible options for dealing with the remarriage of divorced people. The first is the most 'open.' There is a progression down the list of options towards an increasingly 'disciplined' approach.

Another way of explaining the relationship between the five options is to see that Options One and Five are a pair of mirror opposites. Option One says 'yes' to all divorced people, whilst option Five says 'no.' Options Two, Three and Four are three of a kind. Each agrees that there are circumstances where the church can participate in seeking God's blessing on a new relationship. However, how to handle the line between the *biblical* and the *extra-biblical* is what distinguishes them, together with the question of what form of service is appropriate.

Before looking in more detail at each of these Options, and considering the arguments for and against them, I want to draw attention to the 'lines of paradox' at the foot of figure 1.

Lines of Paradox

The first line of paradox is between grace and holiness. Our policy needs to hold together, as best it can, these two seemingly contradictory poles of truth. We need to find some way of proclaiming God's grace, mercy and forgiveness, whilst upholding the high doctrine of the marital bond as taught by Jesus. Remember, so high was Jesus' teaching that the disciples said 'If this is the situation between a husband and wife, it is better not to marry' (Mt 19.10).

The second line of paradox is between the individual and the community. If one was just considering the individual, it might seem right to express the grace of God by offering remarriage. However, the church has a responsibility to the community around it to make a clear stand about the lifelong nature of marriage vows. Certainly, if the church makes no stand about the lifelong nature of those vows, nobody else will.

We turn now to consider the five options as expressed in the table below:

Figure 1: OPTIONS TABLE

Category of Divorce	Biblical	Extra-biblical	Contra-biblical
Option One	Remarry	Remarry	Remarry
Option Two	Remarry	Remarry	Discipline
Option Three	Remarry	Prayer and Dedication	Discipline
Option Four	Prayer and Dedication	Prayer and Dedication	No Service
Option Five	No Service	No Service	No Service

Lines of Paradox

grace ⟷ holiness

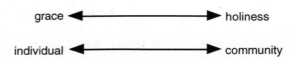

individual ⟷ community

The Five Options: What to Offer to Whom

Option *One* is the offer of marriage to all divorced people who request it. Such an approach certainly solves many problems since little or no 'checking out' has to be done beforehand. It is strong in an emphasis on God's acceptance of those who have experienced the trauma of divorce. However, its emphasis on grace can seem to fall within what Bonhoeffer called 'cheap grace.' It is also weak in what it communicates to the surrounding community (and internally to its own 'community of faith') about the lifelong nature of marriage vows.

Option *Two* seeks to line up with the Scriptures in saying that where divorce has taken place within limits, then there is authority to offer a marriage service. Moreover, the argument goes, the biblical grounds should be seen as 'for example' cases, and not as definitive legal ruling. It is argued, for example, that repeated physical or sexual abuse of spouse or child is a stronger ground for divorce than an isolated instance of adultery.

A variation of options One and Two is the use of a special, and appropriate, penitential introduction to a service of marriage. This is the practice of the Anglican Church of Southern Africa. It overcomes the feeling of the service having an element of pretence, a pretence which arises because what everyone knows as the background to the marriage (namely the divorce of one or both of the partners) is not mentioned. It should be able to handle such an introducing in a way that does not induce guilt in those being married, but rather humility in those who are witnesses to the event ('let him that is without sin cast the first stone').

Option *Three* also sees authority in Scripture for the marriage of those who have been divorced within the *biblical* categories developed in sections three and four above. When it comes to the *extra-biblical* category, the argument is as follows. However much we might sympathize with people in this situation, there is no direct biblical warrant for divorce. It is therefore judged that a marriage service is not the appropriate action to take. Rather, what is offered is a *Service of Prayer and Dedication after Civil Marriage* (hereinafter called simply a *Service of Prayer and Dedication*). The Appendix deals with the theological and practical issues raised by such services.

The weakness of this approach centres around the fact that the policy has three different categories, and—in practice—the more the categories, then the more *grey-area* decisions will emerge in which it is difficult to categorize any particular marriage breakdown. The problems emerge particularly around the drawing of the line between the *biblical* and *extra-biblical* cases.

It is the grey areas which cause the problem, for there is an infinite gradation of certainty. There are, to take the adultery grounds as an example (and the same gradation applies to the 'desertion' and 'new creation' categories), a whole range of different situations. For some, adultery will be the specified ground of divorce on the decree *nisi*. Even there we have to take on trust the assurance of the 'innocent' party that they did not also commit adultery. And if they did, were they the first to sin or not? Already one can see that the 'evidence' is not as black and white as one would like. It becomes increasingly grey. What if adultery was known to have taken place but never admitted? Or what if adultery was suspected but never proved? Was the suspicion well founded, or is it evidence of the need of the 'innocent' to assure themselves of the guilt of the other?

This uncovers a further problem associated with option Three (and, to a lesser extent with option Four) namely that the minister (supposedly acting as a pastor) finds himself acting as judge—and, moreover, judge in a rather unjust court. He is only allowed to hear one side of the case, he cannot compel anyone to give evidence and he has no way of substantiating such evidence as he is given.

Furthermore it cannot be ignored that some groupings are much better at presenting a 'good case' than others. Yet those who are least able to make out a good case are often the more 'honest.' Jesus seemed to side with those who were honest about their failures rather than with those who were good at making out a convincing case for their innocence ('I have not come to call the righteous but sinners to repentance' Lk 5.32). The pastor, in such a situation, could well feel—with Jesus—'who made me a judge or an arbiter between you?' (Lk 12.14).

What is most likely to happen if such a policy is adopted is that people will be given 'the benefit of the doubt' so that the *extra-biblical* category will, in practice, disappear and the great majority will be offered remarriage, with some (in the *contra-biblical* category) refused. It is not being argued that option Three is unworkable, but rather that although it appears as the 'middle way,' the pressure of events is likely to push the policy towards option Two or option Four.

Indeed it is right to point out that options Two and Four do—by a prior definitive decision about what is being offered—have the advantage that they take the focus of concern away from the secondary issue of 'what sort of service will we have?,' and puts attention where it is needed, namely on 'what sort of a marriage will we achieve?'

Option *Four* is the offer of a *Service of Prayer and Dedication* to all within the *biblical* and *extra-biblical* categories. This option has the same strengths and weaknesses as option Two, resulting from reducing the number of categories to two. This makes it a more easily workable option than option Three. Some of the grey-area decisions will remain, though the *contra-biblical* category is easier to identify so the problems are significantly reduced. It does hold the balance between grace and holiness and between the individual and the community better that options *One* and *Five*.

The line between the individual and community is held through not offering a service of marriage. A stand is being made, but by offering a *Service of Prayer and Dedication* a positive response is forthcoming. Compared with option Two this option is weighted more at the *holiness* than *grace* side of that line of paradox.

However, there are weaknesses. One of them concerns the seeming compromise or 'fudge' of the difference between a *Marriage Service* and a *Service of Prayer and Dedication*. We address that question in the Appendix. Our decision in choosing option Four was based on the experience of the *Service of Prayer and Dedica-*

14

tion which team members had, and a conviction that it kept the individual/community balance best in our situation. However, we were well aware that option Four is not as generous, to those divorced within the acknowledged *biblical* grounds, as options Two or Three.

Option *Five* is the mirror image opposite to option One. This is the policy of refusing to marry anyone who has been divorced on the grounds that divorce is perceived to be contrary to the will of God. Here a firm stand within the community is certainly being made (though so 'firm' that it is likely to be seen as judgmental). Grace and mercy are difficult to identify in such an approach. Rather, it is likely to be seen as an expression of the church's desire that the 'problem would go away.' The trouble is that it will not. Such an approach certainly solves the problem of pastoral engagement with the people concerned since the decision has been made before any contact is established. A church adopting such a policy would be likely to find that the surrounding community looked elsewhere not only for ministry to the divorced, but for all spiritual sustenance.

Three Ways of Handling Decisions

We turn now to the question of how decisions are made about which service, and indeed, whether any service is to take place. Here there are three fundamentally different styles that can be used to deal with this. Although options One and Five rule out any such questions, the other three do require decisions to be made. Any one option will look quite different in operation according to who makes the vital decisions and how they are made.

The three styles I have called *Watchman*, *Guidelines*, and *Flexible*. In the Watchman style the couple themselves make the decision. In the Guidelines style the clergy or church leaders make the decisions within agreed criteria. In the Flexible style each case is dealt with 'on its merits.' It is important in deciding a policy about the marriage of the divorced to also decide which of these three styles is going to be adopted. Let us now explore them in more depth. These three styles form, with the five options, a grid or matrix which provides the map we need for making such decisions.

The Watchman Style: Handing Over the Decision

The *Watchman* principle is based on the teaching of the prophet Ezekiel:

'Son of man, I have made you a watchman for the house of Israel; so hear the word I speak and give them warning from me. When I say to the wicked, "O wicked man, you will surely die," and you do not speak out to dissuade him from his ways, that wicked man will die for his sin, and I will hold you accountable for his blood. But if you do warn the wicked man to turn from his ways and he does not do so, he will die for his sins, but you will be saved yourself.' (Ezekiel 33.7-9)

This approach minimizes control over people's lives and maximizes their responsibility for their own behaviour, decisions and lives. It is the same principle that Anglicans often use in relation to the baptism of infants. Parents are required to come to a preparation course or meeting, after which application forms for baptism are handed out. The decision is that of the parents. They have had the 'small print' of what they are committing themselves to explained. Under this principle it is reckoned that the parents are just as likely to 'get it right' as the clergy. In the case of remarriage the conviction would be that the couple were just as likely to get it right as anyone 'sitting in judgment' on them. One of the great advantages of such an approach is that it reduces any sense of the interview with the clergy seeming to be like an examination to pass.

If this were to be adopted, there would need to be an initial interview to identify anyone considered to be in the *contra-biblical* category (though options Two and Three could abolish or ignore the *contra-biblical* category). Such an approach has the advantage of reducing the role of clergy and lay leadership, as judges of others, and puts them—where they see they belong—in a pastoral role.

It would be appropriate to require attendance at a marriage preparation course. However, in view of the very different dynamic involved in second marriages, it would be preferable for a special meeting, course or interview (depending on time and manpower available) to be set up specifically to deal with 'remarriage after divorce.' The material outlined in part three of this booklet could provide the basis of such a course.

The Guidelines Style: Defining the Framework

The *Guidelines* style is based on the approach of the Council of Jerusalem's way of decision-making. When the church made its first major pastoral decision (whether Gentiles could be fully members of the church) the apostles established the principle, in Acts 15, that:

'It seemed good to the Holy Spirit and to us not to burden you with anything beyond the following requirements…' (Acts 15.28)

In other words they established the 'requirements' or rules by which others were to be accepted. Those requirements were as simple, self evident, and objective as possible. Although 'law' was being established, it was shot through with 'grace,' the apostles explaining that they did not want to 'burden you with anything beyond the following requirements…'

We, in fact, chose the Guidelines style rather than the Watchman style since we judged that a stronger pastoral control was appropriate in our situation. Operating in a church with a fairly high 'discipleship culture' made this approach the most appropriate. We ruled out the Flexible style (see next section) as it would have created great problems in a Team Ministry if one staff member was perceived to be more 'flexible' than another.

Having made that decision, we then had to identify what the guidelines were. In doing so we sought to establish as clear and objective biblical principles as we could that were likely to have as high a degree of self-evident justice as was possible. We established the following *pastoral principles* about who we felt able to offer a *Service of Prayer and Dedication* to. The same principles could be used if a *Marriage Service* was offered.

We decided we would be willing to conduct a service where the past and present relationships were being handled in harmony with the teaching of Scripture. Our concern here was not to set impossibly high standards but rather to avoid the scandal of seeking God's blessing on a relationship which is being handled in a way contrary to the will of God. There are four specific, and objective, matters we would want to establish before agreeing to offer a *Service of Prayer and Dedication*. They are:

a) that the person concerned is seeking to come to a place of forgiveness towards the former partner and is not carrying on a continuing vendetta.
   ('Make every effort to live in peace with all men and to be holy; without holiness no one will see the Lord. See to it that no-one misses the grace of God and that no bitter root grows up to cause trouble and defile many.')   *(Heb 12.14,15)*

b) that the person concerned is seeking to deal responsibly with the support of the partner and, especially, the children of the previous marriage.
   ('If anyone does not provide for his relatives, and especially for his immediate family, he has denied the faith and is worse than an unbeliever.')   *(1 Tim 5.8)*

c) that the person concerned is not seeking to marry an unbeliever.
   ('Do not be yoked together with unbelievers.')   *(2 Cor 6.14)*

d) that the couple concerned are not living or sleeping with each other.
   ('But among you there must not be even a hint of sexual immorality, or of any kind of impurity, or of greed, because these are improper for God's holy people.')   *(Eph 5.3)*

Two points need to be made about these standards. First, for Anglican clergy, there is a double standard involved here for it is not legally possible to refuse a first marriage on the grounds that (c) and (d) in the paragraph above are not being observed. We recognize this but would answer that the issue this booklet is dealing with is how to handle requests for a second marriage. In this area it is within an Anglican clergyman's authority to refuse a marriage, and we judge that these tests are appropriate.

The second point concerns the issue of cohabitation. This has been highlighted in the Grove Booklet by Greg Forster, *Marriage before Marriage?* (Ethical Study 69). Others, including the Mothers' Union, have raised questions about the increasing practice of cohabitation. These issues were raised subsequent to the writing of this booklet. The reader is simply referred to this matter which needs more attention than can be given in the space of this booklet.

However, it needs to be recorded that these two issues have been dealt with in a number of cases over more than a decade of pastoral practice. We have been struck by the willingness of Christian couples to hear the case against cohabitation and by their readiness to separate until after their marriage. There have been two instances of couples who objected to such a stance and who left the church with some ill-feeling, though one of those couples has since rejoined the church.

Appropriate time-scales. We would only be willing to consider a request for remarriage from someone who has been involved in the life of the church for at least six months. We would be willing to outline our approach to anyone at any time, but no decision on whether to offer to take a *Service of Prayer and Dedication* would be made until after that six month period. In addition, we would only be willing to offer such a service when two years have elapsed since the separation from the previous partner, and at least one year since the issuing of a decree *nisi*.

Commitment to counselling. We would only be willing to offer such a service where the partner who had been divorced had been through a counselling process designed to help them deal creatively with the past in terms of forgiveness towards the former spouse, receiving forgiveness for themselves and integrating the past experience into their own self-understanding.

The Flexible Style: Deciding Each Case on Its Merits

The *fFexible* style involves taking each case on its merits and having as few (if any) rules about who one will or will not offer a service to (whether a *Marriage Service* or a *Service of Prayer and Dedication*).

There are great attractions to this approach, as the very use of the word 'flexible' indicates. Rules are minimal and people are most likely to feel cared for, listened to, and understood. It makes a merit of making no attempt to develop a policy as this booklet is seeking to do. No immediate decision is required. That is a great attraction to hard-pressed clergy! In a small church and stable community it may be possible to take this approach—at least in the short term.

However, the advantages are not as real as might be hoped. An 'every-case-on-its-merits' approach will inevitably end up establishing a form of 'case law.' In the long run that is likely to be indistinguishable from a *Guidelines* approach.

For example, the first person who comes may admit that they did regularly commit adultery whilst in the previous marriage and would see nothing wrong in doing the same in the new one. The majority of ministers might well be reluctant to offer any service in such circumstances. However, *at the very moment of making that decision* a guideline has been established. Case law is being built up.

What is being argued in this booklet is that, to minimize the confusion among those who come to us, we should have thought through what the 'rules' are. There will still be major pastoral decisions to make as to how to interpret and apply the general rules in specific situations. In other words, you cannot be pastoral without developing rules, and you cannot have rules and yet somehow avoid pastoral implications. The stark alternatives do not exist in reality. The danger is, that whilst seeming to be 'loving' and 'spiritual,' those who say 'we will deal with each case on its merits' may be doing so in the hope that the problem will go away. That is neither pastorally sensible nor sensitive. 'Forewarned is forearmed' in the end proves more loving.

However, this is a style that will commend itself to some. The primary point being made in this booklet is that if we choose this, or either of the other styles, we should do so aware of the strengths and weakness of the style we choose.

Handling Community Requests

The advantage of offering a *Marriage Service* (option Two), linked to the Watchman principle is that 'church and community' are treated alike.

In operating a policy of offering a *Service of Prayer and Dedication*, linked to the Guidelines principle we have had to consider how to respond to requests from non-church members for a remarriage after divorce. Any couple from the community, of whom one had been divorced, who requested remarriage would be informed that our policy is:

a) we do not conduct a *Marriage Service* for those who have been divorced.

b) we do, in certain circumstances, take a *Service of Prayer and Dedication*.

c) a member of staff would be very happy to meet them and explain our policy in more detail, if they wished to discuss their situation further.

If such a meeting is requested we would explain our reasons for the four standards outlined under *Guidelines* above, and would further explain that our concern is to establish marriages in which both partners are seeking to discover God's grace for their life together. We have found that telling people both (a) and (b) above does certainly clarify the situation and minimize building up expectations which will not be fulfilled. We have not so far had anyone who is not a church member, wishing to pursue a *Service of Prayer and Dedication*.

3

Pastoral Issues

As has already been stated, the attention of those who come, wanting to be married in church when one partner has been divorced, is usually on what form of service they will have, rather than what sort of marriage they will achieve. Our task is to help such people give attention to the latter issue.

In the course of our experience the following issues have had to be addressed. Out of them have emerged a number of guidelines which are listed below.

Prevention

We have established the following guidelines whilst recognizing that this is a commitment to a considerable amount of work:

1. *We refuse to be dramatic about marriage problems,* or treat couples going through difficulties as failures in their discipleship. Problems in establishing and sustaining a marriage are signs of life and normality. Refusing to admit that problems exist is a greater threat to a marriage than having difficulties.

2. *We want to encourage members to be open about their marriages* and to share problems at an early stage with appropriate pastoral leaders or counsellors, recognizing the pressures on marriage and family today.
3. *We want to train and equip pastors and counsellors in marriage guidance,* or know professionals in these areas to whom people can be referred.
4. *We want to make marriage preparation and marriage support training widely available within the church.* We are now seeing virtually all couples who come for marriage, taking part in our marriage preparation course (five evenings, at present—but previously a Saturday morning and afternoon).

Separation

We *encourage* separation in circumstances that, without it, would put a partner or children under serious physical, moral or psychological threat.

In all cases of separation we would teach, encourage and help a Christian partner to work for reconciliation, and we would seek to provide resources or contact with outside agencies to that end.

If a separated partner refuses, long-term or after a period of attempting it, to make any further effort in reconciliation, and the pastoral leadership discern that such a refusal stems ultimately from disobedience to God, we need to make our judgment clear and consider what discipline is appropriate.

If the abandoning of attempts at reconciliation stem rather from a recognition that the relationship has irretrievably broken down, then we will seek to help the person cope with the experience of bereavement which accompanies the death of a marriage.

When a Christian partner who is separated wishes to stay in the fellowship and starts another sexual relationship, they would be disciplined as though they were fully married (which they are).

Discipline

Through this booklet there has been reference to a process of discipline, which now needs to be spelt out. It has four stages to it. We aim to have not more than two weeks between any stage. In the last ten years we have taken one or more steps with over one dozen couples. The four stages are as follows:

The first stage is one of *warnings* as outlined in Mt 18.15-20.

The second stage involves removal of someone from whatever *ministry* they currently exercise. It is important for this to be done so as not to give a wrong witness to others both in the church and in the surrounding community.

The third stage involves removal from *fellowship* group. This should be done with an explanation to the fellowship group of why this has been done, and how they should seek to relate to the person. It is part of the Matthew 18 process mentioned above.

The fourth stage involves removal from *communion*. In the Anglican tradition this has to be done with the Bishop's knowledge and indeed legal authorization.

We have normally found that people withdraw themselves from communion without taking formal steps when once the issue has been raised. We have not so far attempted official excommunication.

Repentance

It is important that there are agreed objective tests as to whether repentance has taken place or not ('confession without change is a game'). We consider that repentance has taken place when a person is able to:

1. Recognize that their action was sinful, and have some understanding of the pain that it has caused to God and other human beings.
2. Seek and receive forgiveness both from the offended partner (as far as that partner is willing to do so) and from God.
3. Have a greater and truer self-understanding (rather than projection of wrongs onto the former partner).
4. Be at peace with former partner (in so far as that partner will allow it).
5. Put the needs of any children first should divorce be the long-term result.

Where such repentance is forthcoming, at any stage in the discipline process, then that process is put into reverse since the purpose of discipline is to bring people to order their lives according to God's will.

Counselling Guidelines

Our task is to minister the grace of God to those who have experienced divorce so that they will be free of the past, more mature as people and in their faith, and able to make a new beginning. Our work is to help such people know in their own lives the reality that God is a redeemer who brings good out of evil.

Our attitude to a person who has experienced divorce is not one of judgment (even when wrong has been done by them), but rather a desire to help them deal with the past, integrate the lessons into their present attitude to themselves and others, and move on.

All of us are in the life-long process of becoming whole. It is important, therefore, not to be looking for some unattainable wholeness in a person as a result of this process, but rather a sufficient level of personal honesty to make a new relationship one that can be encouraged rather than discouraged.

What follows is a checklist of points, in note form, to help in counselling.

1. *Help them to a true understanding of the past*
a) being honest about any way in which their actions were sinful and contributed to the breakdown of the marriage. We need to pay attention to:
   - false guilt: which is turning the blame in on self (the most frequent response to divorce since the rejection of love is experienced as rejection of self).
   - denial: the human urge, since the fall, to hide from the truth and God.
   - blaming: scapegoating another person (former partner or third party).

b) being honest about the former partner and their actions.
  - neither scapegoating: and loading all the pain onto the other.
  - nor excusing: and thereby unable to forgive because unable to admit the sin.

2. *Help them to a place of repentance*
  - for any sin on their part
  - then ensure they experience *absolution*. Anointing with oil, and use of the sign of the cross on the forehead are helpful ways of communicating the reality of forgiveness.
  - and are able to experience the 'joy of sins forgiven.'

3. *Help them to a place of forgiveness*
a) first of themselves (often the hardest step)
  - remember it is not possible if sin is not acknowledged in the first place.
  - remember the opposite tendency to blame oneself where there is no sin.
b) second of their partner
  - it is good to help people to speak out forgiveness audibly.
  - remember this is a process (possibly lasting a lifetime) and should not be done glibly.
  - prepare them for the likelihood of needing to repeat this process whenever the symptoms of unforgiveness surface again (probably from a deeper level).
c) third, for any third party.
  - be alert to any unhealthy scapegoating, especially where it is masking a denial of the former partner's responsibilities.

4. *Help them to a greater self-understanding*
  - able to own their weaknesses and limitations and yet accept themselves.
  - able to incorporate this trauma into their lives, through awareness of danger signs in themselves, and by greater acceptance of similar traits in others.
  - able to know God in the valley and dark places: trust him in testing times.

5. *Help them to order the outward circumstances*
a) responsibility to children to be well provided for
  - including not allowing matters of access to become a way of getting back at former partner.
  - or seeking to 'poison' minds of children against former partner.
b) just sharing of resources
  - avoiding 'giving it all away' (a sign of self-rejection and attitude of 'I don't deserve anything, I'm worthless')
  - or 'fighting for every last penny' (a sign of not having forgiven the former partner and so desiring to 'take it out on them')
  - or being too 'spiritual' (for example, not using solicitors).
c) being at peace with former partner
  - it may not be reciprocated, but from this side forgiveness should be ex-

pressed, not in the denial of the sin of the other, but in the releasing of them from any 'debt' or desire to 'make them pay for this.'

6. *Help them to begin a new life in the community*
a) help them through the various stages of the inevitable bereaving process (made worse by fact that former partner is alive)
   - this process includes guilt, denial, anger, acceptance.
   - it is important to allow anger to be owned and expressed (it is not sinful itself, only if clung onto for safety and identity)
b) help them to know God as redeemer
   - he is able to bring good out of evil.
   - we want to get people (without forcing them or the pace) to be able to say with Joseph: 'You meant it for evil, but God meant it for good.'
   - and with Solzhenitsyn 'I turn back to the years of my imprisonment and say…"Bless you prison"…I nourished my soul there. "Bless you, prison, for having been in my life."' (Leanne Payne, *Broken Image* p 154).
c) help them to see and grasp new opportunities.
   - to discover the freedom in singleness and to focus on what they can now do, rather than on what they lack.
   - this may well include a lower standard of living: help them to trust God with their needs, and see the unnecessary nature of some necessities', but beware of glibness, there can be real poverty here.

Appendix

Services of Prayer and Dedication

There are two major objections to a *Service of Prayer and Dedication*.

One objection is that such a service is a legal fiction, pretending to be one thing but actually being another. 'What, in the final issue,' the question runs, is the difference between a *Service of Prayer and Dedication* and a *Marriage Service?*' The answer, at one level is 'very little.' One is a service of blessing in the context of civil marriage, the other is a service of blessing after civil marriage.

This is part of the value of such a service. We cannot be party to any form of 'blessing' (by a service of marriage or a service of Prayer and Dedication) if we do not think God will bless the union. In this way such a service is giving as full a recognition of the new relationship before God as a *Marriage Service*.

However, by not being a normal *Marriage Service* it does signal the uniqueness of first marriages, and the life-long intention of the marriage vows. Those who are witnesses to this second marriage (for at least one of the couple) know that something different is taking place. It expresses more clearly than a second

Marriage Service that the past is not being swept under the carpet.

A further advantage in such services is that it gives freedom to develop an event unique to the particular circumstances of that couple including, where appropriate, the active participation of any children.

The other objection to *Services of Prayer and Dedication* is that they are a 'second class service.' The answer to this objection has to be in actions rather than words. Given the support of the local church, and the creativity of the clergy in developing it, such a service *need not* be second class. This, of course, can only be established as people experience such a service as 'the best' rather than 'second best.' Some options for achieving this goal are spelt out below.

Conducting Services of Prayer and Dedication

What follows is based on the Anglican services booklet *Services of Prayer and Dedication after Civil Marriage*. Almost all of it applies equally to the other denominations who can either adapt this form, use the forms developed by their own denomination, or create their own local patterns of service. The clergy on the St Thomas's staff team who have had experience of such services see them in a very positive light and believe that they have a number of advantages over the use of the normal marriage service. A penitential section introduces the context and there is much greater flexibility to adapt the service to the varied needs of those involved. We identify five possible ways of using this material:

Prayer-meeting mode. There are some who want a quiet and private event. In such cases the Dedication (section 12) could be the central part of a small prayer meeting in the vestry for close friends which would have an extended time of prayer for the couple as the central part of the service.

Wedding-type mode. For the great majority, this would be what they want. This order of service lends itself to such an approach combining liturgy, promises, prayer and worship—the normal ingredients of a wedding service. Sections 1, 2, 3, 12, 14, 15, 18 would form the framework.

Charismatic mode. Some (particularly those from a non-liturgical background) will want to take advantage of the opportunity to break away from the 'formal' feel of a wedding-type service and make a strong celebration out of the service. Worship—Word—Dedication would be a simple order of service.

Eucharistic mode. Section 24 explains how the Dedication can be built into a Communion Service. With its emphasis on penitence at the beginning, and the proclamation of God's power to forgive and redeem expressed in the sacrament, this is a particularly attractive possibility.

Sunday service mode. Along the lines of the practice of the Orthodox church, it would be possible to insert the *Service of Prayer and Dedication* into a Sunday service, such as in the intercessions section of communion. In some situations this could be a very creative way of affirming the couple before the whole church.